INTRODUCING . . .

Piggy

Crocky-Wock

The Lion

Stingaling

The Porcupine

The Ant-eater

Books by Roald Dahl

THE BFG

BILLY AND THE MINPINS

BOY: TALES OF CHILDHOOD

CHARLIE AND THE CHOCOLATE FACTORY

CHARLIE AND THE GREAT GLASS ELEVATOR

THE COMPLETE ADVENTURES OF CHARLIE
AND MR WILLY WONKA

DANNY THE CHAMPION OF THE WORLD

DIRTY BEASTS

THE ENORMOUS CROCODILE

ESIO TROT

FANTASTIC MR FOX

GEORGE'S MARVELLOUS MEDICINE

THE GIRAFFE AND THE PELLY AND ME

GOING SOLO

JAMES AND THE GIANT PEACH

THE MAGIC FINGER

MATILDA

REVOLTING RHYMES

THE TWITS

THE WITCHES

To discover more books, and find out more about
Roald Dahl, please visit the website at **roalddahl.com**

ROALD DAHL

DIRTY BEASTS

Illustrated by **Quentin Blake**

PUFFIN

PUFFIN BOOKS

UK | USA | Canada | Ireland | Australia
India | New Zealand | South Africa

Puffin Books is part of the Penguin Random House group of companies
whose addresses can be found at global.penguinrandomhouse.com.

www.penguin.co.uk   www.puffin.co.uk   www.ladybird.co.uk

First published in the USA by Farrar, Straus and Giroux 1983
First published in Great Britain by Jonathan Cape 1984
Published by Puffin Books 1986
This edition published 2016, reissued 2023

001

Printed in Great Britain by Clays Ltd, Elcograf S.p.A.

The authorized representative in the EEA is Penguin Random House Ireland,
Morrison Chambers, 32 Nassau Street, Dublin D02 YH68

A CIP catalogue record for this book is available from the British Library

ISBN: 978-0-241-56872-9

All correspondence to:
Puffin Books, Penguin Random House Children's
One Embassy Gardens, 8 Viaduct Gardens, London SW11 7BW

Words matter. The wonderful words of Roald Dahl can transport you to different worlds
and introduce you to the most marvellous characters. This book was written many years ago,
and so we regularly review the language to ensure that it can continue to be enjoyed by all today.

Puffin Books would like to thank Inclusive Minds for introducing us to its
network of Inclusion Ambassadors. You can read more about the work
Inclusive Minds does here: www.inclusiveminds.com.

CONTENTS

The Pig   1

The Crocodile   7

The Lion   11

The Scorpion   15

The Ant-Eater   21

The Porcupine   31

The Cow   39

The Toad and the Snail   45

The Tummy Beast   57

THE PIG

In England once there lived a big
And wonderfully **CLEVER** pig.
To everybody it was plain
That Piggy had a **MASSIVE** brain.
He worked out sums inside his head,
There was no book he hadn't read,
He knew what made an airplane fly,
He knew how engines worked and why.

He knew all this, but in the end
One question drove him round the bend:
He simply couldn't puzzle out
What LIFE was really all about.
What was the reason for his birth?
Why was he placed upon this earth?
His **GIANT** brain went round and round.
Alas, no answer could be found,

Till suddenly one wondrous night,

All in a flash, he saw the light.

He jumped up like a ballet dancer

And yelled, **'BY GUM,** I'VE GOT THE ANSWER!

They want my bacon slice by slice

To sell at a tremendous price!

They want my **TENDER JUICY CHOPS**

To put in all the butchers' shops!

They want my pork to make a roast

And that's the part'll cost the most!

They want my sausages in strings!

They even want my **CHITTERLINGS!**

The butcher's shop! The carving knife!

That is the reason for my life!'

Such thoughts as these are not designed

To give a pig great peace of mind.

Next morning, in comes Farmer Bland,

A pail of pigswill in his hand,

And Piggy with a mighty **ROAR,**

Bashes the farmer to the floor . . .

3

Now comes the rather grizzly bit

So let's not make too much of it,

Except that you *must* understand

That Piggy *did eat* Farmer Bland,

He ate him up from head to toe,

Chewing the pieces nice and slow.

It took an hour to reach the feet,

Because there was so much to eat,

And when he'd finished, Pig, of course,

Felt absolutely no remorse.

Slowly he scratched his brainy head

And with a little smile, he said,

'I had a fairly powerful hunch

That he might have me for his lunch.

And so, because I feared the worst,

I THOUGHT I'D BETTER **EAT *HIM* FIRST.'**

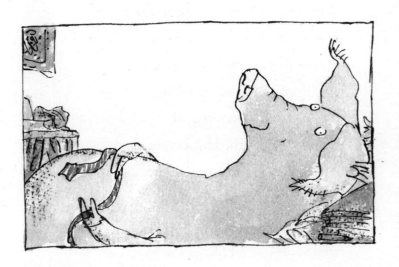

THE CROCODILE

No animal is half so vile
As **CROCKY-WOCK** the crocodile.
On Saturdays he likes to crunch
Six juicy children for his lunch,
And he especially enjoys
Just three of each, three girls, three boys.
He smears the boys (to make them hot)
With mustard from the mustard pot.

But mustard doesn't go with girls,
It tastes all wrong with plaits and curls.
With them, what goes extremely well
Is BUTTERSCOTCH and **CARAMEL**.
It's such a super marvellous treat
When boys are hot and girls are sweet.
At least that's Crocky's point of view.
He ought to know. He's had a few.

That's all for now. It's time for bed.
Lie down and rest your sleepy head . . .
Ssh! *Listen!* What is that I hear
GALLUMPHING softly up the stair?

Go lock the door and fetch my gun!

Go on, child, **HURRY!** QUICKLY, **RUN!**

No, stop! Stand back! He's coming in!

Oh, look, that greasy greenish skin!

The shining teeth, the greedy smile!

IT'S

CROCKY-WOCK,
THE CROCODILE!

THE LION

The lion just adores to **EAT**

A lot of red and tender meat,

And if you ask the lion what

Is much the tenderest of the lot,

He will not say a

ROAST OF LAMB

Or curried beef or

DEVILLED HAM

Or crispy pork or

CORNED BEEF HASH

Or sausages or

MUTTON MASH.

Then could it be a

BIG PLUMP HEN?

He answers no. What is it, then?

Oh, lion dear, could I not make
You happy with a LOVELY STEAK?
Could I entice you from your lair
With **RABBIT-PIE** or **ROASTED HARE?**
The lion smiled and shook his head.
He came up very close and said,
'The meat I am about to chew
Is neither steak nor chops. **IT'S YOU.'**

THE SCORPION

You ought to thank your lucky star
That here at home where you are
You'll never find (or so it's said)
A scorpion inside your bed.
The scorpion's name is **STINGALING,**
A most repulsive ugly thing,
And I would never recommend
That you should treat him as a friend.
His scaly scales are black as black
With armour-plate upon his back.

Observe his scowling murderous face,
His wicked eyes, his lack of grace,
Note well his long and crinkly tail.
And when it starts to SWISH AND FLAIL,

Oh gosh! Watch out! JUMP BACK, I say,
And run till you're a mile away.

The moment that his tail goes SWISH
He has but one determined wish,
He wants to make a sudden JUMP
And sting you hard upon your rump.
'What *is* the matter, darling child?
Why do you look so tense and wild?'
'Oh Mummy, underneath the sheet
There's something moving on my feet,
Some horrid creepy crawly thing,
D'you think it could be **STINGALING?'**
'What **NONSENSE,** child! You're teasing me.'
'I'm not, I'm not! It's reached my knee!
It's going . . . going up my thigh!
Oh Mummy, catch it QUICKLY! TRY!

17

It's on . . . it's on my bottom now!
It's . . .

OW!

OW-OW!

OW-OW!

OW-OW!'

THE ANT-EATER

Some wealthy folks from U.S.A.,

Who lived near San Francisco Bay,

Possessed an only child called **ROY,**

A nasty, sly and horrid boy –

All those who met him soon recoiled,

Because he was most dreadfully spoiled.

Whatever Roy desired each day,

His parents bought him *RIGHT AWAY* –

Toy motor-cars, electric trains,

The latest model aeroplanes,

A colour television set,
A saxophone, a clarinet,
Expensive teddy bears that talked,
And animals that walked and squawked.
(As well as this, young Roy would choose,
Two pairs a week of brand-new shoes.)
And now he stood there shouting, 'What
On Earth is there I haven't got?
How hard to think of something new!
The choices are extremely few!'
Then added, as he scratched his ear,
'Hold it! I've got **A GOOD IDEA!**
I think the next thing I must get
Should be a most peculiar pet –
The kind that no one else has got –
A giant **ANT-EATER!** Why not?'
As soon as father heard the news,
He quickly wrote to all the zoos.
'Dear all,' he said, 'My dear keepers,
Do any of you have ant-eaters?'

They answered by return of mail.

'Our ant-eaters are not for sale.'

Undaunted, Roy's fond parent hurled

More messages across the world.

He said, 'I'll pay you through the NOSE

If you can get me one of those.'

At last he found an Indian fellow

(He lived near Delhi, and played the cello)

Who said that he would sacrifice

His pet for an ENORMOUS price

(The price demanded, if you please,

Was fifty thousand gold rupees).

The ant-eater arrived half-dead.

It looked at Roy and softly said,

'I'm famished. Do you think you could

Please give me just a LITTLE food?

A crust of bread, a bit of meat?

I haven't had a thing to eat

In all the time I was at sea,

For nobody looked after me.'

Roy shouted, **'NO! NO BREAD OR MEAT!**

Go find some ants! They're what you eat!'

The starving creature crawled away.

It searched the garden night and day,

It hunted **EVERY INCH** of ground,

But not one single ant it found.

'Please give me food!' the creature cried.

'Go find an ant!' the boy replied.

By chance, upon that very day,

Roy's father's sister came to stay –

A vicious fiend of eighty-three

Whose name, it seems, was Dorothy.

She said to Roy, 'Come let us sit

Out in the sun and talk a bit.'

Roy said, 'I don't believe you've met

My new and most unusual pet?'

He pointed down among the stones

Where something lay, all skin and bones.

'Ant-eater!' he yelled. 'Don't lie there yawning!

This is my ant! Come say good morning!'

(Most people in the U.S.A.
Pronounce some words a different way
From how an English person might
And usually that's quite all right.
Instead of **AUNT**, they call it **ANT,**
Instead of **CAN'T**, they call it **KANT.)**
Roy yelled, 'Come here, you so-and-so!
My ant would like to say hello!'
Slowly, the creature raised its head.
'D'you mean that that's an *ant*?' it said.

'Of course!' cried Roy. 'Ant Dorothy!
This ant is over eighty-three.'
The creature smiled. Its tummy rumbled.
It licked its starving lips and mumbled,
'A GIANT ANT! By gosh, a *WINNER!*
At last I'll get a decent dinner!
No matter if it's eighty-three.
If that's an ant, then it's for me!'
Then, taking very careful aim,
It *POUNCED* upon the startled dame.
It grabbed her firmly by the hair
And ate her up right then and there,
Murmuring as it chewed the feet,

'The largest ant I'll ever eat.'
Meanwhile, our hero Roy had sped
In terror to the potting-shed,
And tried to make himself obscure
Behind a pile of horse-manure.
But Ant-eater came sneaking in
(Already it was much less thin)
And said to Roy,

'YOU LITTLE SQUIRT,
I THINK I'LL HAVE YOU FOR
DESSERT.'

THE PORCUPINE

Each Saturday I shout HOORAY!
For that's my pocket-money day
(Although it's clearly understood
I only get it when I'm good).
This week my parents had been told
That I had been as GOOD as **GOLD,**
So after breakfast 50p
My generous father gave to me.
Like lightning down the road I ran
Until I reached the sweet-shop man,
And bought the chocolates of my dreams,
A GREAT **BIG** BAG OF RASPBERRY CREAMS.
There is a secret place I know
Where I quite often like to go,
Beyond the wood, behind some rocks,
A super place for **GUZZLING** chocs.

When I arrived, I quickly found

A comfy-looking little mound,

Quite clean and round and earthy-brown

Just right, I thought, for sitting down.

Here I will sit all morning long

And eat until my chocs are gone.

I sat. I screamed. I jumped a foot!

Would you believe that I had put

That tender little rump of mine

Upon a **GIANT** PORCUPINE!

My backside seemed to catch on fire!

A hundred red-hot bits of wire

A hundred prickles sticking in

And puncturing my precious skin!
I ran for home. I shouted, 'MUM!
BEHOLD THE PRICKLES
     IN MY BUM!'
My mum, who always keeps her head,
Bent down to look and then she said,
'I personally am not about
To try to pull *those* prickles out.

I think a job like this requires

The services of Mr Myers.'

I shouted, 'Not the dentist! **NO!**

Oh Mum, why don't *you* have a go?'

I begged her TWICE, I begged her THRICE,

But grown-ups never take advice.

She said, 'A dentist's very strong.

They pull things out the whole day long.'

She drove me quickly into town,

And then they turned me **UPSIDE DOWN**

Upon the awful dentist's chair,

While two strong nurses held me there.

Enter the dreaded Mr Myers

Waving a **MASSIVE** pair of pliers.

'This is,' he cried with obvious glee,

'A new experience for me.

Quite honestly I can't pretend
I've ever pulled things from *this* end.'
He started pulling one by one
And yelling 'My, oh my, what fun!'
I shouted 'Help!' I shouted **'OW!'**
He said, 'It's nearly over now.
For heaven's sake, don't **SQUIRM ABOUT!**
Here goes! The last one's coming out!'
The dentist pulled and out it came,
And then I heard the man exclaim,
'Let us now talk about the fees.
That will be fifty guineas, please.'
My mother is a gutsy sort
And always keen to share her thoughts.
She cried, **'BY GOSH,** that's jolly steep!'
He answered, 'No, it's very cheap.
My dear woman, can't you see
That if it hadn't been for me
This child could go another year
With prickles sticking in her rear.'

So that was that. **OH, WHAT A DAY!**

And what a fuss! But by the way,

I think I know why porcupines

Surround themselves with prickly spines.

It is to stop some silly clown

From squashing them by sitting down.

Don't copy me. Don't be a twit.

Be sure you

LOOK

before you

SIT.

THE COW

Please listen while I tell you now
About a most fantastic cow.
MISS MILKY DAISY
   was her name,
And when, aged seven months,
   she came
To live with us, she did her best
To look the same as all the rest.
But, Daisy, as I will divulge,
Had an unconventional bulge.
A funny sort of **BUMPY** lump
On either side, above the rump.
Now, not so very long ago,
These bumpy lumps began to grow,
And three or maybe four months later,
(I stood there, an enthralled spectator)

These bumpy lumps burst

W I D E   A P A R T

And out there came (I cross my heart)
Of all the wondrous marvellous things,
A pair of gold and silver wings!
A cow with wings! A flying cow!
I'd never seen one up to now.
'Oh Daisy dear, can this be true?'
She flapped her wings and UP SHE FLEW!
Most gracefully she climbed up high,
She fairly whizzed across the sky.
You should have seen her dive and swoop!

She even did a LOOP THE LOOP!

Of course, almost immediately
Her picture was on live TV,

And millions came each day to stare

At Milky Daisy in the air.

They shouted

    'JEEPERS CREEPERS! **WOW!**

It really is a flying cow!'

They laughed and clapped and cheered

   and waved,

And all of them were well-behaved

Except for one quite horrid man

Who had a short attention span.

This fellow, standing in the crowd,

Raised up his voice and yelled aloud,

'That silly cow! Hey, listen, Daisy!

I think you're absolutely crazy!'

Unfortunately Daisy heard

Quite clearly every single word.

'BY GOSH,' she cried, 'what awful cheek!

I don't think that you're one to speak!'

She dived, and using all her power

She got to sixty miles an hour.

'Bombs gone!' she cried. 'Take that!' she said,

And DROPPED a cowpat on his head.

THE TOAD AND
THE SNAIL

I really am most awfully fond
Of playing in the lily-pond.
I take off shoes and socks and coat
And paddle with my little boat.

Now yesterday, quite suddenly,
A giant toad came up to me.
This toad was **EASILY AS BIG**
As any fair-sized fattish pig.
He smiled and said, 'How do you do?
Hello! Good morning! How are you?'
(His face somehow reminded me
Of Mummy's sister Emily.)
The toad said, 'Don't you think I'm fine?
Admire these lovely legs of mine,
And I am sure you've never seen
A toad so GLORIOUSLY green!'
I said, 'So far as I can see,
You look just like Aunt Emily.'
He said, 'I'll bet Aunt Emily
Can't **JUMP** one half as high as me.
Hop on my back, young friend,' he cried,
'I'll take you for a marvellous ride.'
As I got on, I thought, oh blimey,
Oh, deary me. How wet and slimy!

'Sit further back,' he said. 'That's right.
I'm going to jump, so hold on tight.'
He **JUMPED!** Oh, how he **JUMPED!** By gum,
I thought my final hour had come!
My wretched eardrums popped and fizzed.
My eyeballs watered. Up we whizzed.
I clung on tight. I shouted, 'How
Much further are we going now?'
Toad said, his face all wreathed in smiles,
'With every jump, it's fifty miles!'
Quite literally, we jumped all over,
From Scotland to the Cliffs of Dover!
Above the Cliffs, we stopped for tea,
And Toad said, gazing at the sea,
'What do you say we take a chance,
And jump from England into France?'
I said, 'Oh dear, d'you think we oughta?
I'd hate to finish in the **WATER.'**
But toads, you'll find, don't give a wink
For what we little children think.

He didn't bother to reply.
He jumped! You should have seen us **FLY!**

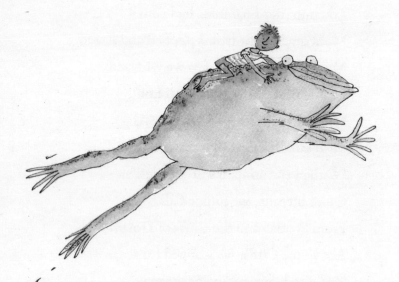

We simply **SOARED** across the sea,
The marvellous Mister Toad and me.
Then down we came, and down and down,
And landed in a brand-new town.

We landed hard, in fact we bounced.

'We're there! It's France!' the Toad announced.

He said, 'You must admit it's grand

To jump into a foreign land.

No boats, no bicycles, no trains,

No cars, no noisy aeroplanes.'

Just then, we heard a fearful shout,

'OH, HEAVENS ABOVE!'

   the Toad cried out.

I turned and saw a frightening sight –

On every side, to left, to right,

People were running down the road,

Running at me and Mister Toad,

And every person, man and wife,

Was brandishing a carving knife.

It didn't take me very long

To figure there was something wrong.

And yet, how could a small boy know,
For nobody had told me so,
That Frenchmen aren't like you or me,
They do things very differently.
They won't say 'yards', they call them 'metres',
And they're the *most peculiar* eaters:
A Frenchman frequently regales
Himself with half-a-dozen SNAILS!
The greedy ones will gulp a score
Of these foul brutes and ask for more.
(In many of the best hotels
The people also eat the shells.)
Imagine that! My stomach turns!
One might as well eat slugs or worms!
BUT WAIT. READ ON A LITTLE BIT.
You haven't heard the half of it.
The French go even more agog
If someone offers them a FROG!
(You'd better fetch a basin quick
In case you're going to be sick.)

The bits of frog they like to eat
Are THIGHS and CALVES
and TOES and FEET.

The French will gobble loads and loads
Of legs they chop off frogs and toads.
They think it's absolutely ripping
To guzzle frogs-legs fried in dripping.
That's why the whole town running for their lives
Were rushing us with carving knives.
They screamed in French, 'Well I'll be blowed!
What legs there are upon that toad!
CHOP THEM! SKIN THEM!
COOK THEM! FRY THEM!
All of us are going to try them!'
'Toad!' I cried. 'I'm not a funk,
But ought we not to do a bunk?
These rascals haven't come to greet you.
All they want to do is eat you!'

Toad turned his head and looked at me,

And said, as cool as cool could be,

'Calm down and listen carefully please,

I often come to France to tease

These hungry French who long to eat

My lovely tender froggy meat.

I am a **MAGIC TOAD!'**   he cried.

'And I don't ever have to hide!

Stay where you are! Don't move!' he said,

And pressed a button on his head.

At once, there came a blinding flash,

And then the most almighty crash,

And sparks were bursting all around,

And smoke was rising from the ground . . .

When all the smoke had cleared away

The French folk with their knives cried, *'HEY!*

Where is the toad? Where has he gone?'

You see, I now was sitting on

A wonderfully **ENORMOUS** SNAIL!

His shell was smooth and brown and pale,
And I was so high off the ground
That I could see for miles around.
The Snail said, 'Hello! Greetings! Hail!
I was a Toad. Now I'm a Snail.
I had to change the way I looked
To save myself from being cooked.'
'Oh Snail,' I said, 'I'm not so sure.
I think they're starting up once more.'
The French were shouting, 'What a snail!
Oh, what a monster! What a whale!
He makes the toad look titchy small!
There's lovely snail-meat for us all!
We'll bake the creature in his shell
And ring aloud the dinner-bell!
Get garlic, parsley, butter, spices!
We'll cut him into fifty slices!
Come sharpen up your carving-knives!
This is the banquet of our lives!'
I murmured through my quivering lips,

'Oh Snail, I think we've had our chips.'

The Snail replied, 'I disagree.

Those greedy French, they'll not eat me.'

But on they came. They screamed,

Surround the brute and run him through!'

Good gracious, I could almost feel 'YAHOO!

The pointed blades, the shining steel!

But Snail was cool as cool could be.

He turned his head and winked at me,

And murmured, '*Au revoir*, farewell,'

And pulled a lever on his shell.

I looked around. The Snail had **GONE!**

And *now* who was I sitting on? . . .

Oh what relief! What joy! Because

At last I'd found a friend. It was

The gorgeous, glamorous, absurd,
Enchanting **ROLY-POLY BIRD!**
He turned and whispered in my ear,
'Well, fancy seeing you, my dear!'
Then up he went in glorious flight.
I clutched his neck and hung on tight.
We fairly raced across the sky,
The Roly-Poly Bird and I,
And landed safely just beyond
The fringes of the lily-pond.
When I got home I never told
A solitary single soul
What I had done or where I'd been
Or any of the things I'd seen.

I did not even say I rode
Upon a **GIANT** JUMPING TOAD,
'Cause if I had, I knew that they
Would not believe me anyway.
But you and I know well it's true.
We know I **JUMPED,** we know I flew.
We're sure it all took place, although
Not one of us will ever know,
We'll never, never understand
Why children go to **WONDERLAND.**

THE TUMMY BEAST

One afternoon I said to Mummy,
'Who is this person in my tummy?
He must be SMALL and very THIN
Or how could he have gotten in?'
My mother said from where she sat,
'It isn't nice to talk like that.'
'It's **TRUE!**' I cried. 'I swear it, Mummy!
There *is* a person in my tummy!

He talks to me at night in bed,

He's always asking to be fed,

Throughout the day, he screams at me,

Demanding sugar buns for tea.

He tells me it is not a sin

To go and raid the **BISCUIT TIN.**

I know quite well it's awfully wrong

To **GUZZLE** food the whole day long,

But really I can't help it, Mummy,

Not with this person in my tummy.'

'You horrid child!' my mother cried.

'Admit it right away, you've lied!

You're simply trying to produce

A silly asinine excuse!

You are the greedy guzzling brat!

And that is true!' she loudly spat.

I tried once more, '*Believe* me, Mummy,

There is a person in my tummy.'

'I've had enough!' my mother said,

'You'd better go at once to bed!'

Just then, a nicely timed event

Delivered me from punishment.

Deep in my tummy something stirred,

And then an awful noise was heard,

A **SNORTING**

GRUMBLING

GRUNTING sound

That made my tummy jump around.

My darling mother nearly died,

'My goodness, what was that?' she cried.

At once, the tummy voice came through,

It shouted, 'Hey there! Listen, you!

I'm getting hungry! I want eats!

I want **LOTS** of **CHOCS** and **SWEETS!**

Get me half a pound of **NUTS!**

Look snappy or I'll twist your guts!'

'That's him!' I cried. *'He's in my tummy!*

So now do you believe me, Mummy?'

But Mummy answered nothing more,

For she had FAINTED on the floor.

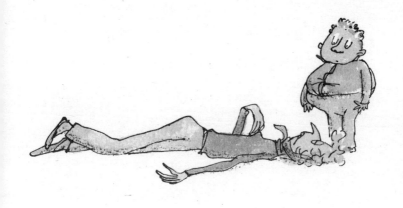

LET'S FIND OUT
HOW **CAREFULLY** YOU
WERE READING . . .

1. **WHAT DOES CROCKY-WOCK LIKE TO PUT ON CHILDREN BEFORE HE EATS THEM?**
   a. Butterscotch, caramel and mustard
   b. Cream and sprinkles
   c. Tomato ketchup

2. **WHERE DOES STINGALING LIKE TO BITE?**
   a. On the bottom
   b. On the ear
   c. On the toe

3. **WHO HAS TO PULL THE PORCUPINE'S SPIKES OUT?**
   a. The doctor
   b. The dentist
   c. The vet

4. **WHAT DOES DAISY THE COW DROP FROM THE SKY?**
   a. A pie
   b. A rock
   c. A cowpat

5. **WHAT COUNTRY DOES THE TOAD VISIT?**
   a. Germany
   b. America
   c. France

ANSWERS: 1. a. 2. a. 3. b. 4. c. 5. c.

What a **HORRIBLE** lot of **BEASTS** in these poems! Surely there can't be any more out there? Read on to find out . . .

REVOLTING RHYMES

JACK AND THE BEANSTALK

Jack's mother said, 'We're *stony broke*!
Go out and find some wealthy bloke
Who'll buy our cow. Just say she's sound
And worth at least a hundred pound.
But don't you dare to let him know

THAT SHE'S AS *OLD* AS BILLY-O.'

Jack led the old brown cow away,
And came back later in the day,
And said, 'Oh, mumsie dear, guess what
Your clever little boy has got.
I got, I really don't know how,
A super trade-in for our cow.'
The mother said, 'You little creep,
I'll bet you sold her much too cheap.'

When Jack produced one lousy bean,
His startled mother, turning green,
Leaped high up in the air and cried,
'I'm *absolutely stupefied*!
YOU SILLY BOY! D'you really mean
You sold our Daisy for a bean?'
She snatched the bean. She yelled,
    'You chump!'
And *F L U N G* it on the
    rubbish dump.
At ten p.m. or thereabout,
The little bean began to sprout.
By morning it had grown so tall
You couldn't see the top at all.
Young Jack cried, 'Mum, admit it now!
It's better than a rotten cow!'
The mother said, 'Not so quick!
Where are the beans that I can pick?
There's not *one bean*! It's bare as bare!'

'No no!' cried Jack.

'YOU LOOK **UP** THERE!

Look very high and you'll behold
Each single leaf is solid gold!'
By gollikins, the boy was right!
Now, glistening in the morning light,
The mother actually perceives
A mass of lovely golden leaves!
She yells out loud, 'My sainted souls!
I'll sell the Mini, buy a Rolls!
Don't stand and gape, you little clot!
Get up there quick and grab the lot!'
Jack was nimble, Jack was keen.
He scrambled up the mighty bean.
Up up he went without a stop,
But just as he was near the top,
A ghastly frightening thing occurred –
Not far above his head he heard

A big deep voice, a *RUMBLING* thing
That made the very heavens ring.
It shouted loud,

'FEE FI FO **FUM,**

I SMELL
**THE BLOOD
OF AN
ENGLISHMAN!'**

Jack was frightened, Jack was *QUICK,*
And down he climbed in half a ***TICK.***
'Oh mum!' he gasped. 'Believe you me
There's something nasty up our tree!'

ROALD DAHL STORY DAY

13 SEPTEMBER

EVERY SEPTEMBER, together with our fans across the world, we **CELEBRATE** our FAVOURITE **ROALD DAHL STORIES,** CHARACTERS and WORLDS!

FIND OUT MORE AT
www.roalddahl.com

That's it.
The end of the book.

HERE IS
one LAST **WORD,**
invented by **Roald Dahl** HIMSELF.
Make sure you KEEP IT SAFE.

DADDLE

Verb: To run very fast.

ROALD DAHL